MYSTERY RIDDLES FOR KIDS

200 Easy and Hard Riddles For Kids And Their Families To Solve about fruits, colors, animals, instrument and anything else

Mahdi Amini

Copyright © 2023 Mahdi amini All rights reserved

No part of this book may be reproduced, or stored in a retrieval system, or transmitted in any form or by any means, electronic, mechanical, photocopying, recording, or otherwise, without express written permission of the publisher.

Cover design by: Canvas

Introduction

Welcome, dear readers! If you're seeking a thrilling escape into the world of scary stories for kids and adults or if you're in the market for beautifully designed notebooks, I invite you to visit my author page. It's your gateway to a realm of chilling narratives and exquisite stationery. Thank you "Mahdi Amini"

Contents

Riddles

1. I'm a colorful arc after the rain, but I'm not a rainbow. What am I?

2. I'm a little nut that's hard to crack, but I'm not a joke. What am I?

3. I'm made of paper and come in all colors, but I'm not a flag. What am I?

4. I'm a fluffy white blanket that falls from the sky, but I'm not snow. What am I?

5. I have hands but can't clap, and I point to numbers all day. What am I?

6. I'm the first thing you wear after a bath, but I'm not clothes. What am I?

7. I'm a tiny, glowing speck high in the night sky, but I'm not a star. What am I?

8. I have keys but open no doors, and you press my buttons to type. What am I?

9. I'm a sweet treat with a stick, but I'm not a lollipop. What am I?

10. I'm a big red vehicle that helps put out fires, but I'm not a fire hydrant. What am I?

11. I'm a furry creature that purrs but isn't a cat. What am I?

12. I'm a container with a lid that holds your lunch, but I'm not a refrigerator. What am I?

13. I'm a musical instrument you strum, but I'm not a guitar. What am I?

14.   I'm a green plant that's prickly, but I'm not a cactus. What am I?

15.   I'm a cozy place to sleep, but I'm not a bed. What am I?

16.   I'm a small, winged insect that buzzes around flowers. What am I?

17.   I'm a ring of metal that holds your keys, but I'm not a doorbell. What am I?

18.   I'm a rubbery toy that bounces and comes in many colors, but I'm not a ball. What am I?

19.   I'm a book filled with adventures and stories, but I'm not a library. What am I?

20.	I'm a shiny, round object you hang on the tree, but I'm not an ornament. What am I?

21.	I'm a tool you use to write or draw, but I'm not a pencil. What am I?

22.	I'm a sweet drink made from fruit, but I'm not juice. What am I?

23.	I'm a place where you learn about history and art, but I'm not a museum. What am I?

24.	I'm a small creature that hops and hides, but I'm not a frog. What am I?

25.	I'm a button you press to make a call, but I'm not a phone. What am I?

26.   I'm a giant bird that doesn't fly, but I'm not an ostrich. What am I?

27.   I'm a slippery surface where you glide, but I'm not ice. What am I?

28.   I'm a magical stick that grants wishes, but I'm not a wand. What am I?

29.   I'm a treasure chest with jewels and gold, but I'm not a pirate. What am I?

30.   I'm a tool with teeth that cut through wood, but I'm not a saw. What am I?

31.   I'm a small object that makes your work disappear with a click. What am I?

32.   I'm a cozy place with cushions and pillows, but I'm not a bed. What am I?

33.   I'm a fruit that's yellow on the outside and white on the inside. What am I?

34.   I'm a tiny creature that spins silk, but I'm not a spider. What am I?

35.   I'm a piece of furniture that you sit on, but I'm not a chair. What am I?

36.   I'm a bright light in the night sky, but I'm not the moon. What am I?

37.   I'm a colorful toy that makes music when you press my keys. What am I?

38.   I'm a juicy red fruit that's often found in a pie. What am I?

39.   I'm a place in the house where you cook delicious meals. What am I?

40.   I'm a piece of clothing that covers your hands when it's cold. What am I?

41.   I'm a shiny object you use to cut paper, but I'm not scissors. What am I?

42.   I'm a reptile that's long and scaly, but I'm not a snake. What am I?

43.   I'm a vehicle with two wheels that you ride, but I'm not a bicycle. What am I?

44.   I'm a small creature that hides in a shell, but I'm not a turtle. What am I?

45.   I'm a place filled with colorful flowers and buzzing insects. What am I?

46.   I'm a small bird with a bright red chest, but I'm not a robin. What am I?

47.   I'm a game where you try to find a hidden object. What am I?

48.   I'm a musical instrument with black and white keys, but I'm not a piano. What am I?

49.   I'm a tasty frozen dessert that comes in a cone. What am I?

50.   I'm a room filled with books and knowledge. What am I?

51.I'm a small fish that glows in the dark, but I'm not a goldfish. What am I?

52.   I'm a vehicle that carries many people and travels on tracks. What am I?

53.   I'm a small bug that hops and chirps at night. What am I?

54.   I'm a device that takes pictures, but I'm not a camera. What am I?

55.   I'm a tree with needles and cones, but I'm not a pine tree. What am I?

56.   I'm a tool used to write or draw, but I'm not a pen. What am I?

57.   I'm a small, colorful bird that hums and sips nectar. What am I?

58.   I'm a game with numbers and cards, and you play it with friends. What am I?

59.   I'm a place in the playground with swings and slides. What am I?

60.   I'm a container with a handle, and I keep your drinks hot. What am I?

61.   I'm a yellow fruit that's a favorite of curious monkeys. What am I?

62.   I'm a tiny vehicle that travels on tracks and carries people underground. What am I?

63.   I'm a small reptile with a hard shell, but I'm not a turtle. What am I?

64.   I'm a musical instrument that you blow into to make beautiful tunes. What am I?

65.   I'm a spinning toy that you launch with a string. What am I?

66.   I'm a place where you go to see wild animals from around the world. What am I?

67.   I'm a flying insect that buzzes around and makes sweet honey. What am I?

68.   I'm a piece of sports equipment used to hit a ball over a net. What am I?

69.   I'm a shiny object in the night sky that twinkles and makes wishes come true. What am I?

70.   I'm a fluffy dessert made from egg whites and sugar, often with added flavors and colors. What am I?

71. I'm a mode of transportation that can be found in water, often with paddles. What am I?

72. I'm a creature with feathers and a beak, but I'm not a bird. What am I?

73. I'm a round object that bounces and can be dribbled on a court. What am I?

74. I'm a type of dog that's often associated with herding sheep. What am I?

75. I'm a room filled with screens and speakers for watching movies and shows. What am I?

76. I'm a sweet, frozen treat on a stick that comes in various fruity flavors. What am I?

77.I'm a place where you can see paintings, sculptures, and other works of art. What am I?

78. I'm a type of insect that produces light, often found in warm, humid climates. What am I?

79. I'm a mode of transportation with two pedals and a chain, perfect for a leisurely ride. What am I?

80. I'm a container often used to keep your homemade soup hot. What am I?

81. I'm a playful pet with soft fur and a long tail, known for chasing laser lights. What am I?

82.   I'm a popular board game where you buy and trade properties. What am I?

83.   I'm a fruit that's both red and sour, often used to make tasty pies. What am I?

84.   I'm a small device that stores and plays your favorite songs and podcasts. What am I?

85.   I'm a plant with juicy, spiky leaves often used in soothing gels. What am I?

86.   I'm a sweet, fluffy dessert, but I'm not cotton candy. What am I?

87.   I'm a bird with colorful feathers, often kept as a pet, and known for talking. What am I?

88.   I'm a popular card game where you match numbers and colors to win. What am I?

89.   I'm a vehicle that glides on ice, often used for figure skating and ice hockey. What am I?

90.   I'm a room filled with shelves of board games and puzzles, a perfect place to play. What am I?

91.   When you have me, you want to share me. Once you share me, you don't have me. What am I?

92.   The more you take, the more you leave behind. What am I?

93.   I'm not alive, but I can grow; I don't have lungs, but I need air. What am I?

94.   I'm tall when I'm young and short when I'm old. What am I?

95.   You can see me in water but I never get wet. What am I?

96.   I speak without a mouth and hear without ears. I have no body, but I come alive with the wind. What am I?

97.   I'm not alive, but I can die. I'm not solid, but I can melt. What am I?

98.   I'm a place where secrets are kept, but I'm not a locked room. I'm a keeper of stories, but I'm not a librarian. What am I?

99. I'm a path that leads to a hidden place where your thoughts come to life. What am I?

100. I'm always hungry, I must always be fed. The finger I touch will soon turn red. What am I?

101. I'm taken from a mine, and shut up in a wooden case, from which I'm never released, and yet I am used by almost every person. What am I?

102. I'm not alive, but I can grow; I don't have lungs, but I need air; I don't have a mouth, but water kills me. What am I?

103. I have keys but open no locks, I have space but no room, you can enter, but you can't go inside. What am I?

104.   The more you take, the more you leave behind. What am I?

105.   I'm always hungry, I must always be fed. The finger I touch, soon turns red. What am I?

106.   I'm a word of letters three, add two, and fewer there will be. What am I?

107.   I speak without a mouth and hear without ears. I have no body, but I come alive with the wind. What am I?

108.   I'm never seen but widely known. I'm heard but cannot speak. I'll reveal the truth within you, but I'm not alive. What am I?

109.   I'm a word of letters three, two, and one. I am something that's read from both ends. What am I?

110.   I'm light as a feather, yet the strongest man can't hold me for much longer than a minute. What am I?

111.   I can travel around the world while staying in one corner. What am I?

112.   I have keys but can't open any locks, and I can enter through a closed door. What am I?

113.   I am taken from a mine and shut up in a wooden case, from which I am never released, and yet I am used by almost every person. What am I?

114.   I'm a word of letters three, add two, and fewer there will be. What am I?

115.   I'm not alive, but I can die if you drop me. I'm not solid, but I can melt. What am I?

116.   I am something you can hold in your left hand but not in your right hand. What am I?

117.   I'm not a bird, but I can fly without wings. What am I?

118.   I have cities but no houses, forests but no trees, and rivers but no water. What am I?

119.   I have keys but can't open locks. I have space but no room. You can enter, but you can't go inside. What am I?

120.   I can be cracked, made, told, and played. What am I?

Mahdi amini

Instrument

121.   I have keys but can't open locks, I produce melodies that soothe and shock. What am I?

122.   I'm small and portable, with strings that hum, Strummed by your hand, I make music come. What am I?

123.   I have pipes and keys, but I'm not a door, I create tunes you can't ignore. What am I?

124.   I'm often found in a marching band, I'm held in the hand, but not in the land. What am I?

125.   With holes and keys, I'm made of wood, I'm played by blowing, and I sound so good. What am I?

126.   I'm brass and bold, with valves to press, My sound is loud, you can't suppress. What am I?

127.   I'm like a small piano, with fewer keys, Held in your hand, I'm a musical tease. What am I?

128.   I'm a stringed instrument with a bow to draw, My melodies are sweet, and I have no flaw. What am I?

129.   I'm a percussion instrument with a jingle and shake, I'm often found in a Latin groove to make. What am I?

130.   I'm a wooden box with a skin on top, When you strike me, the beat won't stop. What am I?

Musical

131. I'm fragile as glass, with notes that sway,Tunes in my heart, I play all day.No fingers, yet melodies I bring,What am I, with a sound like a king?

132. I'm tall and grand, a sight to behold, Books galore, their stories untold. Silent whispers in a palace of prose, What am I, where knowledge flows?

133. I come with the night, a shining ball, Guarding the dreams, both big and small. Lunar beauty in the sky so high, What am I, as the stars say goodbye?

134. I'm full of colors, a visual delight, Capturing life with every sight. Frames and moments, forever preserved, What am I, where memories are conserved?

135.	I spin and twist, an enigma's grace,
A puzzling path that you must embrace.
Locked and tangled, a brain's endeavor,
What am I, a mind's challenge forever?

136.	In the realm of kings, I'm poised to strike, White and black, a warlike sight. Pawns and knights in strategy's thrall, What am I, where grand battles install?

137.	I'm an old tale, often in verse, A classic yarn, rehearsed rehearse. Star-crossed lovers, a tragic score, What am I, the Bard's explore?

138.	I'm silent and dark, a cinema's demand, With reels of stories, I take my stand. Images flicker, a world portrayed, What am I, where movies are played?

139.   I'm not alive, but I measure time, Ticking away, a rhythmic chime. My hands move, but I'm never awake, What am I, on the wall for your sake?

140.   I'm a canvas vast, colors run wild, Brushes dance, an artist's child. Masterpieces born with each stroke's zest, What am I, where creativity's expressed?

141.   I'm woven with threads but not made for clothes, You'll lie on me, not wear me to pose. I'm found on a bed where dreams take flight, What am I, providing comfort at night?

142.   I'm sharp and sleek, designed for your aid, With letters and numbers, a screen that's displayed. You tap and you swipe, with tasks to complete, What am I, making life fast and neat?

143.　I'm in the air, but I'm not a breeze, I help you rise with great ease. Inflatable and floating, I bring lots of fun, What am I when the summer's begun?

144.　I'm tiny and round, no bigger than a bean, Turn my pages to find adventures unseen. I'm filled with stories, both old and brand new, What am I, providing worlds to pursue?

145.　I hang from branches but I'm not a leaf, I'm a shiny, small object, a symbol of belief. On festive trees, I glisten and gleam, What am I, bringing holiday's dream?

146.　I have a mouth but can't taste a thing, My hand may spin, a roulette's swing. A game of chance, with numbers in rows, What am I, where fortune bestows?

147.   I'm sweet and fruity, blended with care, In a cup or a glass, a sip to bear. I'm not a smoothie, though I'm quite close, What am I, the elixir you chose?

148.   I'm a room where you sleep, but not the main bed, More compact, and cozy, I'm often widespread. A resting place when the night takes hold, What am I, where dreams are unrolled?

149.   I'm not a phone, but I've got numbers galore, You press my buttons, what I'm used for. I'm not a keyboard, yet keys are my friends, What am I, on which the data transcends?

150.   I am quiet, I do not make a sound, In a library's realm, I'm often found. I'm filled with knowledge, books of all kind, What am I, expanding the mind?

Mahdi amini

37

colors

151.   I'm the color of the sky on a clear day, and the ocean waves that come your way. What color am I?

152.   I'm the color of ripe tomatoes and stop signs, a bold hue that catches your eye. What color do you see?

153.   I'm the color of grass beneath your feet, the leaves on trees that can't be beat. What color is this?

154.   I'm the color of the sun at dawn, and a juicy fruit, so bright and warm. What color might I be?

155.   I'm the color of eggshells and fresh snow, a pure and pristine shade, you know. What color is this?

156.   I'm the color of rich, dark chocolate, a sweet treat that many crave. What color are we talking about?

157.   I'm the color of a ripe banana, a mellow shade that's quite cheerful. What color is it?

158.   I'm the color of the night sky, sprinkled with stars that twinkle and shine. What color can you see?

159.   I'm the color of lavender and violets, delicate and often associated with calm. What color is this?

160.   I'm the color of a warm, sandy beach, where the sun's rays are always in reach. What color am I?

fruits

161.   What fruit is yellow and curved, often eaten at breakfast or as a snack?

162.   What small red fruit is a favorite in desserts and is often used to make jam?

163.   What fruit is green on the outside but has sweet and juicy flesh?

164.   What fruit is often sliced and served in a salad, known for its green skin and black seeds?

165.   What citrus fruit is known for its sour taste and is used to make lemonade?

166.   What fruit is considered the "king of fruits," with a strong smell and spiky green exterior?

167.   What small, blue fruit is often found in pies and pancakes?

168.   What tropical fruit has a hard shell and sweet, white flesh?

169.   What fruit is long and yellow, a close relative of the banana, and is typically cooked before eating?

170.   What small, red fruit is often used to make jelly or juice?

171.   What citrus fruit has a sweet and tangy flavor and is used to make marmalade?

172.   What fruit is known for its tart taste and is often used to make pies and other desserts?

173.   What fruit is green, crunchy, and is often used as a base for salads?

174.   What tropical fruit is yellow and spiky on the outside, with sweet, juicy flesh?

175.   What small, round fruit can be red or yellow and is often eaten fresh or in jams?

176.   What tropical fruit is often found in smoothies, has a soft, creamy texture, and a green skin?

177.   What type of fruit is often called a "stone fruit" and comes in varieties like Bing and Rainier?

178.   What tropical fruit has a spiky skin and sweet, white flesh?

179.   What fruit is known for its purple skin and is often found in a popular pie?

180.   What fruit is often sliced and served on cereal or yogurt, and is bright orange in color?

45

animal

181.   What animal has black and white stripes and is known for its distinctive waddle?

182.   I'm the king of the jungle, and I roar with might. What am I?

183.   I'm known for my hump and can go for a long time without water. What am I?

184.   I'm a bird known for delivering babies in folk tales. Who am I?

185.   I have a long neck and legs, and I can run very fast. What am I?

186.   I'm a marsupial from Australia, known for hopping. What am I?

187.   I'm a reptile known for changing my color and pattern. What am I?

188.	I'm the largest mammal on Earth and feed on tiny plankton. What am I?

189.	I'm a bird that mimics sounds, and I'm often kept as a pet. Who am I?

190.	I'm a marine mammal, known for balancing a ball on my nose. What am I?

191.	I have a spiral horn on my head and I'm often associated with unicorns. What am I?

192.	I'm a nocturnal bird of prey that can rotate my head 270 degrees. What am I?

193.	I'm a small, furry rodent that's a popular pet. Who am I?

194.	I'm a reptile with a hard shell and often live to be very old. What am I?

195.   I'm a large cat known for my beautiful mane. What am I?

196.   I'm a marine animal with eight long arms and a soft body. What am I?

197.   I'm a domesticated animal that goes "moo." Who am I?

198.   I'm a bird that's often associated with wisdom. Who am I?

199.   I'm a slow-moving reptile with a protective shell. What am I?

200.   I'm a tropical bird known for my vibrant colors. What am I?

49

Answers

1. Waterfall

2. A puzzle

3. Crayon

4. Clouds

5. A clock

6. Towel

7. Firefly

8. Computer keyboard

9.   Popsicle

10.   Firetruck

11.   A dog

12.   Lunchbox

13.   Ukulele

14.   Pineapple

15.   Sleeping bag

16. **Butterfly**

17. **Keychain**

18. **Rubber duck**

19. **Storybook**

20. **Tinsel**

21. **Marker**

22. **Smoothie**

23. **School**

24.   Rabbit

25.   Elevator button

26.   Penguin

27.   Water slide

28.   Magic wand

29.   Treasure chest

30.   Ax

31.   Computer Mouse

32.   Couch

33.   Banana

34.   Silkworm

35.   Sofa

36.   Star

37.   Xylophone

38.   Cherry

39.   Kitchen

40. Gloves

41. Paper cutter

42. Lizard

43. Scooter

44. Hermit crab

45. Garden

46. Cardinal

47. Hide and seek

48. **Keyboard**

49. **Ice cream**

50. **Library**

51. **Firefly**

52. **Train**

53. **Cricket**

54. **Smartphone**

55. **Fir tree**

56.   Pencil

57.   Hummingbird

58.   Card game

59.   Playground

60.   Thermos

61.   Banana

62.   Subway

63.   Tortoise

64.   Flute

65.   Yo-yo

66.   Zoo

67.   Bee

68.   Tennis racket

69.   Star

70.   Cotton candy

71.   Canoe

72.   Pelatypus

73.   Basketball

74.   Border Collie

75.   Theater

76.   Popsicle

77.   Art gallery

78.   Firefly

79.   Bicycle

80.   Thermos

81.   Cat

82.   Monopoly

83.   Rhubarb

84.   MP3 player

85.   Aloe vera

86.   Marshmallow

87.   Parrot

88. Uno

89. Ice skate

90. Game room

91. Secret

92. Footsteps

93. A balloon

94. A candle

95. Reflection

96. Echo

97. Ice

98. Diary

99. Imagination

100. Fire

101. Pencil lead/graphite

102. Ice

103. Keyboar

104. Footsteps

105. Fire

106. Few

107. An echo

108. A mirror.

109. Eye

110. Your breath

111. A stamp

112. A key

113. A pencil

114. Few

115. A bowling ball

116. Right han

117. Time

118. A map

119. A keyboard.

120.   A joke

121.   A piano.

122.   A guitar.

123.   An organ.

124.   A drum.

125.   A flute.

126.   A trumpet

127.   A harmonica

128.   A violin

129.   A maraca

130.   A drum.

131.   A music box

132.   A library

133.   The moon

134.   A photo album

135.   A labyrinth

136. A chessboard

137. Romeo and Juliet

138. A projector

139. A clock

140. An art studio

141. A mattress.

142. A smartphone.

143. A balloon.

144. A book.

145. An ornament.

146. A roulette wheel.

147. A fruit juice.

148. A bunk bed.

149. A calculator.

150. A bookshelf.

151. Blue

152. Red

153. Green

154. Orange

155. White

156. Brown

157. Yellow

158. Black

159. Purple

160. Beige

161. Banana

162. Strawberry

163. Watermelon

164. Kiwi

165. Lemon

166. Durian

167. Blueberry

168. **Coconut**

169. **Plantain**

170. **Cranberry**

171. **Orange**

172. **Rhubarb**

173. **Cucumber**

174. **Pineapple**

175. **Cherry**

176. **Kiwi**

177. **Cherry**

178. **Lychee**

179. **Eggplant (also known as aubergine)**

180. **Apricot**

181. **Penguin**

182. **Lion**

183. Camel

184. Stork

185. Giraffe

186. Kangaroo

187. Chameleon

188. Blue Whale

189. Parrot

190. Seal

191. Narwhal

192. Owl

193. Hamster

194. Tortoise

195. Lion

196. Octopus

197. Cow

198. Owl

199.   Turtle

200.   Parrot